W9-CND-455

Where on Earth are Forests?

Bobbie Kalman

Crabtree Publishing Company

www.crabtreebooks.com

Created by Bobbie Kalman

For Ron and Lita Clavier,
who have added friendship and culture to our lives

Author and Editor-in-Chief
Bobbie Kalman

Editor
Kathy Middleton

Proofreader
Crystal Sikkens

Photo research
Bobbie Kalman

Design
Bobbie Kalman
Katherine Berti
Samantha Crabtree

Prepress technician
Katherine Berti

Print and production coordinator
Margaret Amy Salter

Illustrations
Barbara Bedell: pages 12, 15, 20 (left)
Katherine Berti: page 20 (top right)
Bonna Rouse: page 8 (top right)
Margaret Amy Salter: pages 21, 30

Photographs
Corel: page 14 (bottom)
Digital Vision: page 26 (bottom)
iStockphoto: page 31 (bottom)
Shutterstock: Nina B: page 13 (bottom right); Sergey Uryadnikov: page 24 (bottom)
Thinkstock: pages 4 (bottom), 8 (top left), 10–11 (background), 12–13 (background), 13 (bottom left), 28, 29 (background), 30–31 (background), 31 (top)
Wikimedia Commons: Mark Gurney: page 30 (middle left)
All other images by Shutterstock

Library and Archives Canada Cataloguing in Publication

Kalman, Bobbie, author
        Where on Earth are forests? / Bobbie Kalman.

(Explore the continents)
Includes index.
Issued in print and electronic formats.
ISBN 978-0-7787-0500-0 (bound).--ISBN 978-0-7787-0504-8 (pbk.).--
ISBN 978-1-4271-8229-6 (pdf).--ISBN 978-1-4271-8225-8 (html)

        1. Forests and forestry--Juvenile literature. I. Title. II. Series:
Explore the continents

SD376.K35 2014   j333.75   C2014-900888-0
                                         C2014-900889-9

Library of Congress Cataloging-in-Publication Data

Kalman, Bobbie.
  Where on earth are forests? / Bobbie Kalman.
        pages cm. -- (Explore the continents)
  Includes index.
  ISBN 978-0-7787-0500-0 (reinforced library binding : alkaline
paper) -- ISBN 978-0-7787-0504-8 (paperback : alkaline paper) --
ISBN 978-1-4271-8229-6 (electronic-pdf) -- ISBN 978-1-4271-8225-8
(electronic-html)
  1. Forests and forestry--Juvenile literature. 2. Trees--Juvenile
literature. I. Title.
  SD376.K35 2014
  634.9--dc23
                                         2014004889

Crabtree Publishing Company
www.crabtreebooks.com   1-800-387-7650

Printed in the USA/052014/SN20140313

Published in Canada
Crabtree Publishing
616 Welland Ave.
St. Catharines, Ontario
L2M 5V6

Published in the United States
Crabtree Publishing
PMB 59051
350 Fifth Avenue, 59th Floor
New York, New York 10118

Published in the United Kingdom
Crabtree Publishing
Maritime House
Basin Road North, Hove
BN41 1WR

Published in Australia
Crabtree Publishing
3 Charles Street
Coburg North
VIC 3058

Contents

What are forests?

Forests are **biomes**. A biome is a natural area where certain plants grow. A biome also includes the animals that live in that environment. Biomes have different amounts of sunlight and water. They also have different **climates**. Climate is the usual weather in an area. It includes wind, temperature, and **precipitation**, such as rain or snow.

In some forests, it rains every day. In others, it rains during certain times of the year.

Where do forests grow?

Forests grow on six **continents** on Earth. They provide people and animals with food and **habitats** in which to live. Trees also give us clean air to breathe (see page 30). Forests grow in different areas on Earth and at different **altitudes**, or heights, such as high on mountaintops. Forests that grow in hot parts of the world near the **equator** are not the same as those that grow in areas with cold winters. The equator is an imaginary line around the center of Earth.

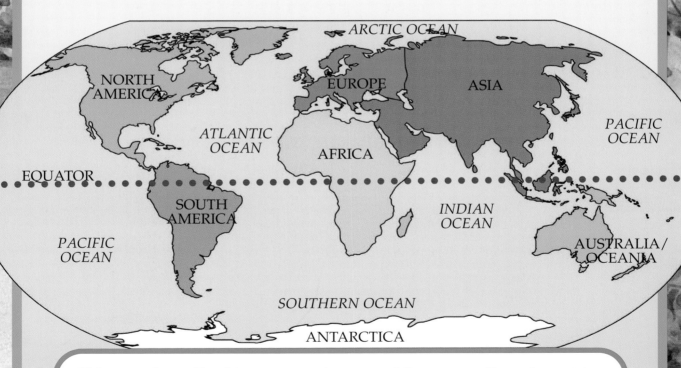

This map shows Earth's seven continents and five oceans. From largest to smallest, the continents are Asia, Africa, North America, South America, Antarctica, Europe, and Australia/Oceania. What are the names of the oceans?

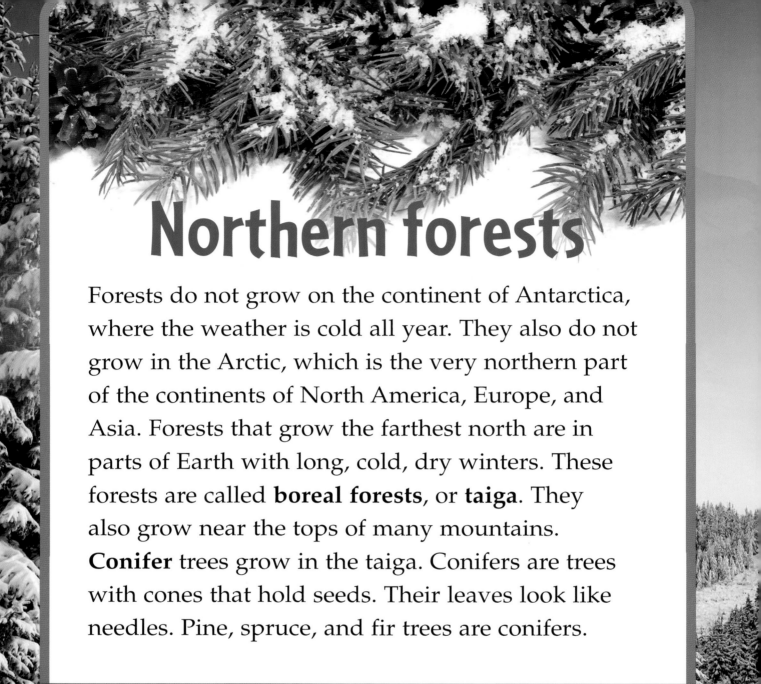

Northern forests

Forests do not grow on the continent of Antarctica, where the weather is cold all year. They also do not grow in the Arctic, which is the very northern part of the continents of North America, Europe, and Asia. Forests that grow the farthest north are in parts of Earth with long, cold, dry winters. These forests are called **boreal forests**, or **taiga**. They also grow near the tops of many mountains. **Conifer** trees grow in the taiga. Conifers are trees with cones that hold seeds. Their leaves look like needles. Pine, spruce, and fir trees are conifers.

This squirrel is sitting on a conifer in a taiga forest. It eats the seeds in the cones of conifers.

Squirrels, moose, reindeer, black bears, wolves, owls, and lynxes are some animals that live in the taiga. This Canada lynx has a thick fur coat to keep it warm during the cold winters.

Conifers grow close together. They form a **canopy**, or large umbrella, over the land. This canopy soaks up the sun.

Temperate forests

In **temperate** areas with mild winters, some forests are made up of conifers and others are made up of **broadleaved** trees. Broadleaved trees have wide leaves with veins. In warm parts of the world, broadleaves stay green all year. In temperate areas with four seasons, broadleaves turn color and drop off the trees in autumn. Trees that shed their leaves are called **deciduous** trees. **Mixed forests** have both conifers and broadleaved trees.

vein

Some broadleaved trees turn color in autumn, and their leaves fall off the trees. This girl is holding a yellow maple leaf. What colors are the other fallen leaves?

Mixed forests with conifers and broadleaved trees are found in areas with four seasons. The leaves of the conifers in these mountain forests have stayed green, but the broadleaved trees are different colors. These deciduous broadleaved trees will soon lose their leaves.

Tropical rain forests

Tropical rain forests are located near the equator on every continent except Europe and Antarctica. They receive at least 100 inches (254 cm) of rain each year. In some tropical rain forests, it rains every day. Other tropical rain forests have a **wet season** and a **dry season**. During the wet season, a lot of rain falls. In the dry season, it may not rain for months.

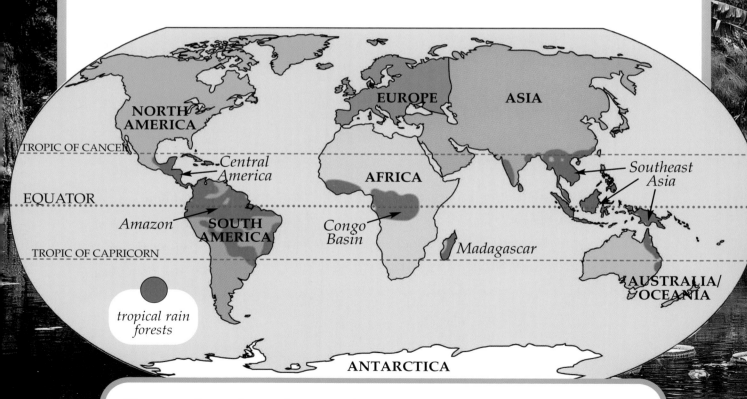

*The map above shows the tropical rain forests on Earth, marked in red. The rain forests are in the **tropics**, which are areas close to the equator, between the imaginary lines of the Tropic of Cancer and the Tropic of Capricorn.*

The largest rain forest

The Amazon Rainforest is the largest tropical rain forest on Earth. It is located in South America, in the countries of Peru, Colombia, Venezuela, Bolivia, Ecuador, Guyana, Suriname, and French Guiana. More than half of this rain forest, however, is in Brazil. The equator runs through the Amazon.

VENEZUELA
GUYANA
SURINAME
COLOMBIA
FRENCH GUIANA
EQUATOR
ECUADOR
Amazon Rainforest
PERU
BRAZIL
BOLIVIA
Amazon Rainforest
CHILE
PARAGUAY
URUGUAY
PACIFIC OCEAN
ARGENTINA
ATLANTIC OCEAN

*The Amazon Rainforest is very important to Earth. One-fifth of the **oxygen** on Earth is produced by the trees of this rain forest.*

*Outside the Amazon, rain forests are also found on the **coasts** and in other parts of South America. Coasts are areas of land near oceans. Two oceans touch South America. What are they? Find them on this map.*

The Amazon Rainforest

emergent

canopy

understory

forest floor

Millions of **species**, or types, of animals live in the Amazon Rainforest. Different animals live in the different layers of the forest. The layers are called **emergent**, **canopy**, **understory**, and **forest floor**. The emergent layer is at the top and is made up of the tallest trees. Below these are the trees in the canopy, where many monkeys live. Shaded by the taller trees, the understory is a cool, dark place where small trees and bushes grow. The forest floor is the ground. Many insects live on the forest floor.

This giant anteater looks for insects to eat on the forest floor.

This spider monkey is sitting at the top of a tall tree in the emergent layer of the Amazon Rainforest.

This toucan lives in the canopy layer. Its huge, colorful beak scares away **predators**.

Margays are small wild cats that live in the trees of the dark understory level of the forest.

Many **indigenous**, or native, people, like these children, live in villages in the Amazon forest.

North American forests

In winter, some animals, like this brown bear, go into a deep sleep. On warmer days, they wake up and look for food in the snowy forests.

Different kinds of forests can be found in North America. Taiga, or boreal forests, grow in Alaska and in the northern parts of Canada, where the winters are long and cold. Mixed forests, containing conifers and deciduous trees, grow in the temperate areas of North America, with four seasons. Farther south, where the weather is always warm, tropical rain forests grow.

Bobcats, also called lynxes, live in mixed forests. Some live in the taiga high on mountains.

Sequoia National Forest is located on the Sierra Mountains in California. Giant sequoias are conifers. They are the tallest and largest trees on Earth.

These black bears live in the taiga in Canada. The mother and her cubs have climbed high on a conifer.

Tropical North America

The southern parts of North America include the state of Florida, the Caribbean Islands, Mexico, and Central America. These areas have a tropical climate, with no real winter. Central America is a strip of land that connects North America to South America, but it is considered part of North America. Tropical rain forests grow in the Central American countries of Costa Rica, Honduras, Belize, and Panama. Capuchin monkeys, howler monkeys, sloths, jaguars, and many species of birds, snakes, and frogs live in these forests.

GREENLAND

ALASKA (USA)

CANADA

UNITED STATES

FLORIDA

CARIBBEAN ISLANDS

BELIZE

MEXICO

CENTRAL AMERICA

HONDURAS

COSTA RICA

PANAMA

SOUTH AMERICA

Capuchin monkeys live in the rain forests of Central America and South America.

This three-toed sloth lives high in rainforest trees in Costa Rica.

This jaguar lives in a rain forest in Belize.

The forests of Europe

Taiga and temperate forests are two kinds of forests that grow on the continent of Europe. Taiga forests are found in the northern parts of Europe, where the winters are very long and cold. Temperate forests grow farther south. Deer, squirrels, foxes, birds, and many other animals live in temperate forests. Europe has no true tropical rain forests because this continent is far from the equator.

Foxes live in temperate forests, as well as in the taiga. This red fox lives in a taiga forest high on a mountain. The winters are cold there.

The Black Forest in Germany is made up of dark pines that grow close together. The trees are such a dark shade of green that the forest looks black from a distance. Most of the Black Forest grows on mountains.

Roe deer also live in both temperate and taiga forests. They feed mainly on grass, leaves, and berries.

The forests of Asia

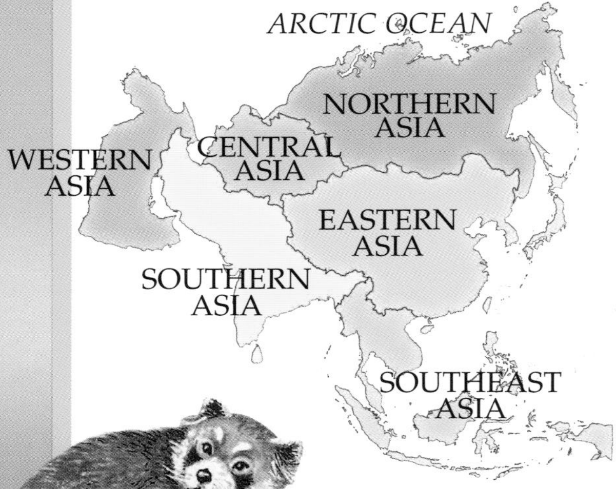

ARCTIC OCEAN

NORTHERN ASIA

WESTERN ASIA

CENTRAL ASIA

EASTERN ASIA

SOUTHERN ASIA

SOUTHEAST ASIA

Asia is the biggest continent. Part of it is near the Arctic, and part is at the equator. Asia is so big that it has been grouped into six **regions**, or areas. Asia has taiga forests, mixed forests, and rain forests.

These brown bears live in the taiga in northern Asia. They eat leaves, fruit, small animals, fish, and large insects.

Mixed forests grow in the warmer parts of Asia that have four seasons. This forest in Northern Asia has both conifers and broadleaved trees.

Bamboo forests grow in Southern Asia, Southeast Asia, and Eastern Asia. Bamboo plants are tall plants that look like trees. They are the largest kinds of grasses. Giant pandas eat bamboo.

Amur tigers are the largest cats. They live in the temperate forests of Eastern Asia. Amur tigers are **endangered**. There are only about 300 to 400 of these cats living in the wild.

Southeast Asia forests

The tropical rain forests in Southeast Asia are some of Earth's oldest forests. In these forests, a lot of rain falls during the rainy season from May to September and then none during the rest of the year. Tropical rain forests are located on many islands near the equator, such as Indonesia, Thailand, and Malaysia. Hundreds of thousands of different animal species live there. Unfortunately, these rain forests also have the greatest number of endangered animal species.

Fewer than 60 Javan rhinoceroses are left. They were once hunted for their horns, which were used to make medicines. This rhino and its calf, or baby, live in a park where hunting is not allowed.

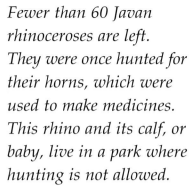

These orangutans live on the island of Borneo. They are endangered because their forest homes are being cut down to be used as farmland. Some orangutans are hunted for their meat, and many babies are captured to be sold as pets.

There are fewer than 400 Sumatran tigers left in the wild. Much of the rain forest where they live has been cut down. Indonesia has set aside parks to help save the tigers that still remain, but many are being killed by **poachers**. Poachers are illegal hunters.

Komodo dragons live on Komodo Island as well as on some other islands in Indonesia. Farmland is taking over their forest homes, and some komodo dragons are being hunted.

African rain forests

Africa is the second-largest continent. Its tropical rain forests are on the west side of Africa in the Congo River Basin and on the island of Madagascar. The Congo Basin contains the second-largest rain forest in the world, after the Amazon. More than 1,000 bird species, 400 mammal species, and 10,000 plant species live there. The Congo Basin also provides food, water, materials, and shelter for over 75 million people.

This man is going into the rain forest to find food.

Forest elephants

The elephants on this page are forest elephants. People once thought that elephants that lived in forests were the same as **savanna** elephants, but they are different. Forest elephants are smaller. They have rounded ears, long jaws, and straight tusks. Forest elephants live in the Congo Basin and in other rain forests in Africa.

Endangered animals

Some endangered animals that live in African rain forests are forest elephants, chimpanzees, gorillas, bonobos, and pygmy hippos. The forests where they live are being cut down and replaced with huge farms. When forests are cut down, animals have no place to live or food to eat. Wild animals, such as monkeys, antelope, and pygmy hippos are also killed for their meat by poachers. The meat is sold in big markets.

Chimpanzees are apes that live in African rain forests. They lose their homes when forests are cut down. They are also hunted illegally for their meat.

All gorillas are endangered, but mountain gorillas are among the most endangered animals in the world. Fewer than 380 of these gorillas live in the Virunga Rainforest in the Congo, shown in the background picture.

The greatest threat to pygmy hippopotamuses is loss of habitat. They are also hunted for their meat.

All lemurs are endangered. Lemurs are **endemic** to Madagascar, which means they can only be found there. Madagascar is a big island that is part of Africa. This black-and-white ruffed lemur lives high up in rainforest trees.

Australia and Oceania

Australia is the smallest continent on Earth and is completely surrounded by water. It is part of a large area called Oceania, which includes thousands of islands. New Zealand, Tahiti, and Fiji are islands that are part of Oceania.

Rain forests near coasts

Tropical rain forests grow in the northern part of Australia and along its coasts. The forests are shown in green on this map.

*Australia's largest **temperate rain forest**, the Tarkine, is on the island of Tasmania. It is home to many endangered animals, like the Tasmanian devil.*

Tasmanian devil

Only in Australia

Koalas are animals called **marsupials**. They live in forests and eat only the leaves of eucalyptus trees. Eucalyptus trees grow mainly in Australia. There are over 600 types, but koalas eat only the leaves of two or three eucalyptus species.

Unlike other kangaroos, which hop along the ground, tree kangaroos live high up in trees in the tropical rain forests of Australia and on some islands in Oceania.

Why we need forests!

sunlight

oxygen

carbon dioxide

water

Trees clean the air. They use sunlight to make food from water and a gas in air called **carbon dioxide**. They let off oxygen, a gas that people and animals need to breathe. Making food using sunlight is called **photosynthesis**.

Saving animals

Forests are home to many kinds of plants and animals. Scientists believe there are more that have not yet been discovered. By saving forests, we also save many species of plants and animals.

The olinguito is a new animal that was discovered in South American forests in 2013. It belongs to the raccoon family.

Keep soil in place

When soil is carried away by wind or water, deserts form, where very few plants can grow. Tree roots hold soil in place so this will not happen.

Explore a forest!

These children are walking through a temperate rain forest. Is there a forest near your home that you could explore with your parents? You can learn more about temperate rain forests at this website: *www.marietta.edu/~biol/biomes/temprain.htm*

Learn more

Learn more about other kinds of forests and what you can do to help preserve them at: *http://eschooltoday.com/forests/forest-preservation-tips-for-kids.html* One way to help is to plant trees. You can also raise money to protect rain forests and teach others why forests are important to all living things.

Glossary

Note: Some boldfaced words are defined where they appear in the book.

continent One of Earth's seven huge areas of land

endangered Describing a plant or animal that is in danger of dying out in the wild

equator An imaginary line around the center of Earth, where it is hot all year

habitat The area or environment in which a certain plant or animal lives

marsupial A type of animal that is born at an early stage and finishes growing inside its mother's pouch

poacher A person who hunts and kills animals against the law

precipitation Any form of water, such as rain or snow, which falls to the Earth's surface

predator An animal that hunts and eats other animals

savanna A grassy plain that is often treeless and is located in tropical areas

temperate rain forest A forest that grows in an area with a mild climate and which gets a lot of rain

tropics Areas with a hot, wet climate that are close to the equator

Index